ROCK RAIDERS

Written by Anna Knight • Illustrated by Roger Harris

Bandit

Chief

Sparks

Axle

Docs

Jet

SAVE THE SPACESHIP

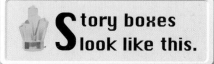

Story boxes look like this.

Puzzle boxes look like this.

Read the story and solve the puzzles on every page.
Can you solve all the puzzles and save the spaceship?
Turn to the answers at the back of the book to see.

A DK Publishing Book
www.dk.com

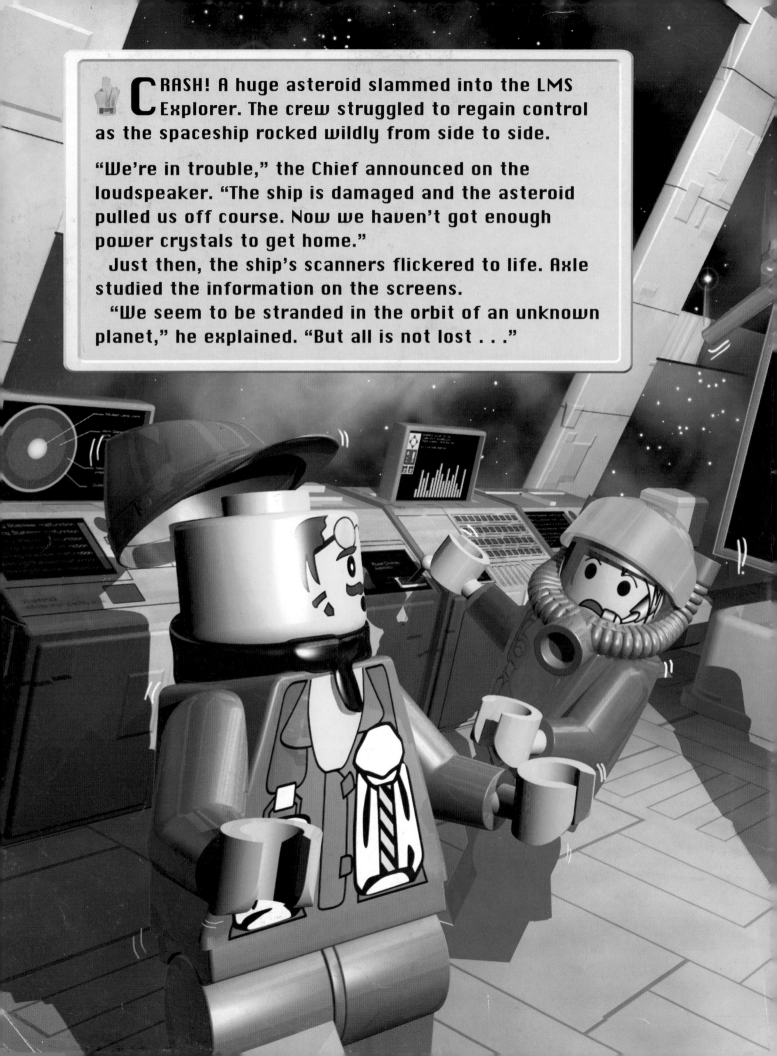

CRASH! A huge asteroid slammed into the LMS Explorer. The crew struggled to regain control as the spaceship rocked wildly from side to side.

"We're in trouble," the Chief announced on the loudspeaker. "The ship is damaged and the asteroid pulled us off course. Now we haven't got enough power crystals to get home."

Just then, the ship's scanners flickered to life. Axle studied the information on the screens.

"We seem to be stranded in the orbit of an unknown planet," he explained. "But all is not lost . . ."

10,000 miles

Outer surface, various elements

Granite

Power crystals

Volcanic rock

LEGO ore

THE FIRST PUZZLE
According to the scanner, what material can be found at 8,000 miles below the surface? At 4,000 miles below the surface?

The Chief sounded worried. "We'll need LEGO ore to repair the spaceship, and power crystals for fuel to get home. There are deposits of ore and crystals on the planet, but we need those resources here on the Explorer."

"I'll take a team of Rock Raiders down to the planet," volunteered Commander Docs. "We'll bring back the resources that we need."

"I guess it's our last hope," said the Chief.

"Only 37 units of power left," calculated Docs. "We need 11 units to keep the ship going, three for every team member going to the planet, plus an extra unit each for their equipment and 6 units to transport the vehicles."

THE SECOND PUZZLE
How many team members can be transported down to the planet?

As a geologist, Commander Docs had expert knowledge that would be vital on this mission. He chose only the best and bravest crew members for his team.

With her experience as an ace pilot, Jet was Docs's first choice. Sparks the engineer had a clever mind covered by a mop of red hair. Bandit the navigator loved sailing and even had a pirate's bushy beard. Last, but not least, Docs chose Axle as the driver.

"There seems to be a sub-surface two miles below ground," said Docs, once Jet had landed the support ship on the planet surface. "It will take us ten seconds to get there in the Tunnel Transporter."

THE THIRD PUZZLE
How fast can the Tunnel
Transporter travel?

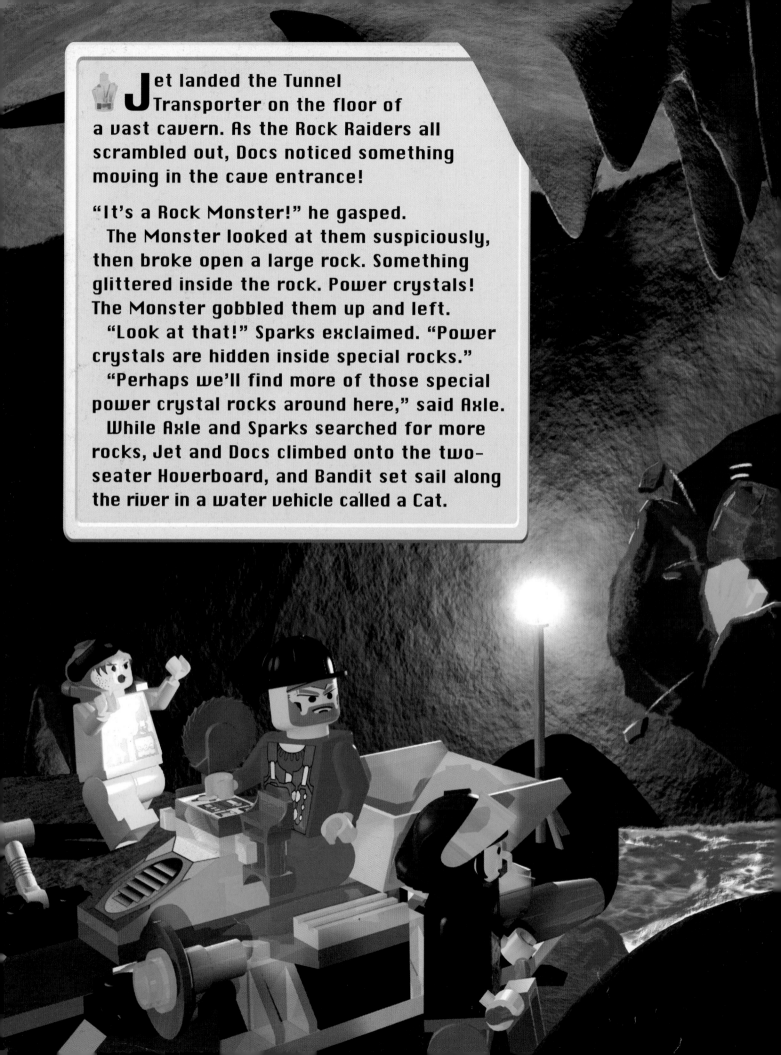

Jet landed the Tunnel Transporter on the floor of a vast cavern. As the Rock Raiders all scrambled out, Docs noticed something moving in the cave entrance!

"It's a Rock Monster!" he gasped.
  The Monster looked at them suspiciously, then broke open a large rock. Something glittered inside the rock. Power crystals! The Monster gobbled them up and left.
  "Look at that!" Sparks exclaimed. "Power crystals are hidden inside special rocks."
  "Perhaps we'll find more of those special power crystal rocks around here," said Axle.
  While Axle and Sparks searched for more rocks, Jet and Docs climbed onto the two-seater Hoverboard, and Bandit set sail along the river in a water vehicle called a Cat.

THE FOURTH PUZZLE
How many power crystal rocks can you find in the picture?

Bandit followed the river through a twisting tunnel. As he turned a corner, the air suddenly grew cold and spiky icicles hung down into the cave.

Bandit's scanner warned of an alien nearby. Suddenly, an ice monster reared up out of the water and threw a sharp spear of ice at him. Bandit swerved. The ice spear missed him and plunged into the water.

"To escape the ice monster, I'll have to go through those rapids," Bandit muttered. "Well, here goes!"

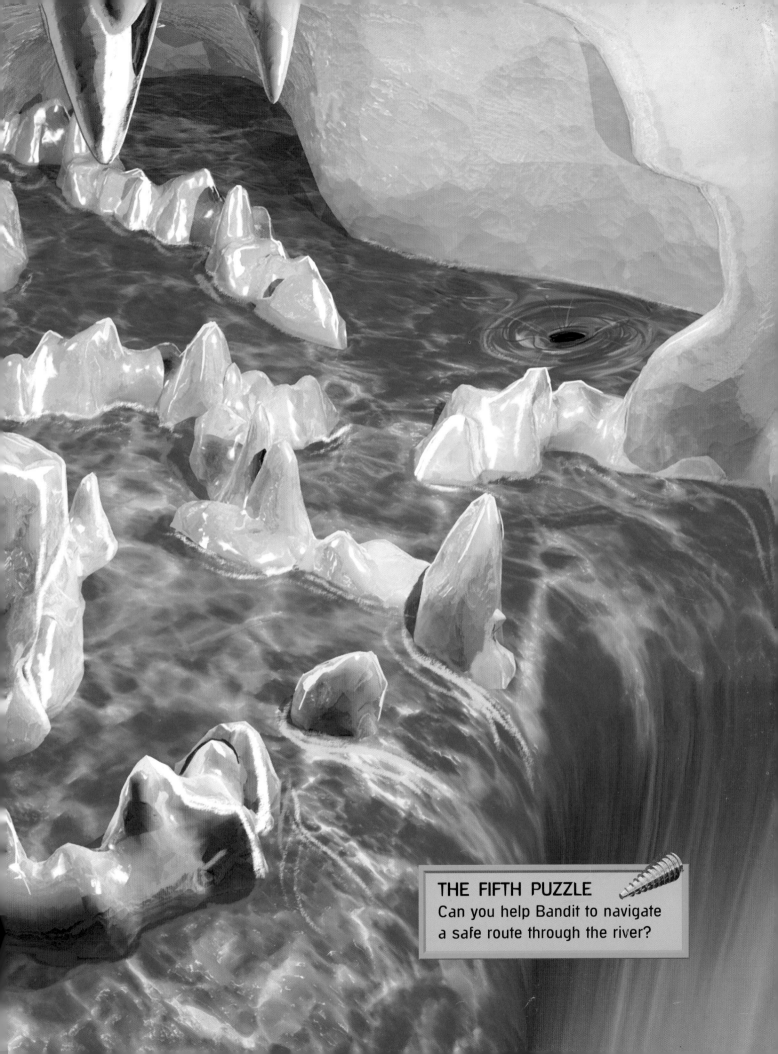

THE FIFTH PUZZLE
Can you help Bandit to navigate a safe route through the river?

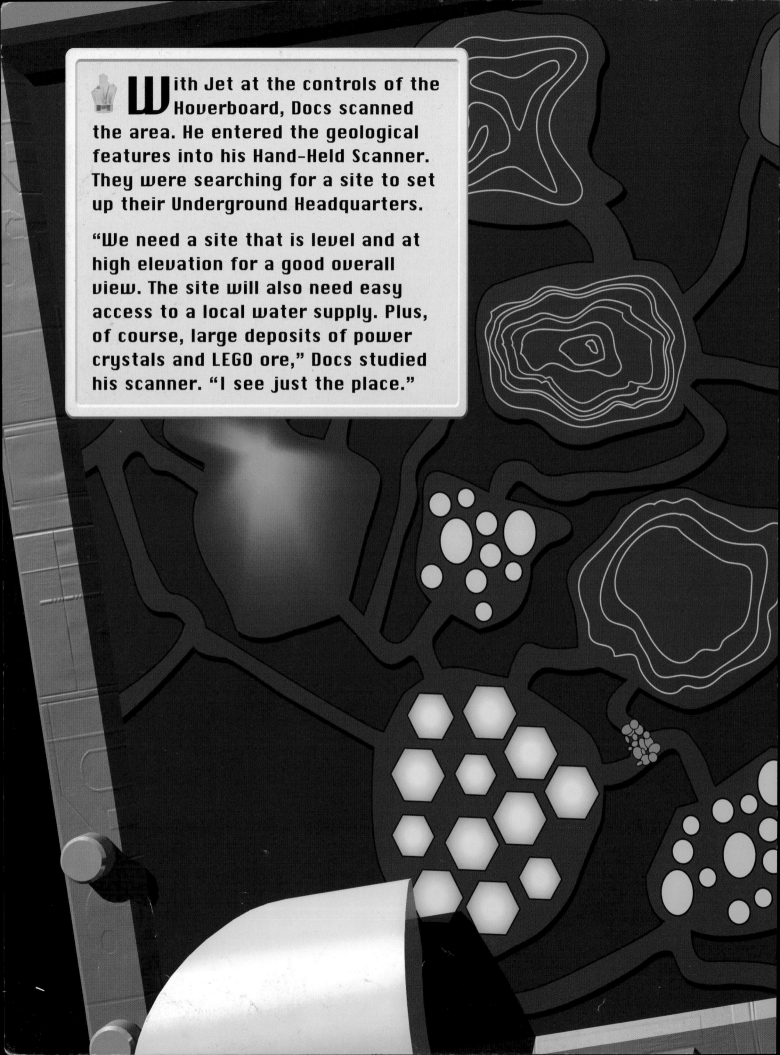

With Jet at the controls of the Hoverboard, Docs scanned the area. He entered the geological features into his Hand-Held Scanner. They were searching for a site to set up their Underground Headquarters.

"We need a site that is level and at high elevation for a good overall view. The site will also need easy access to a local water supply. Plus, of course, large deposits of power crystals and LEGO ore," Docs studied his scanner. "I see just the place."

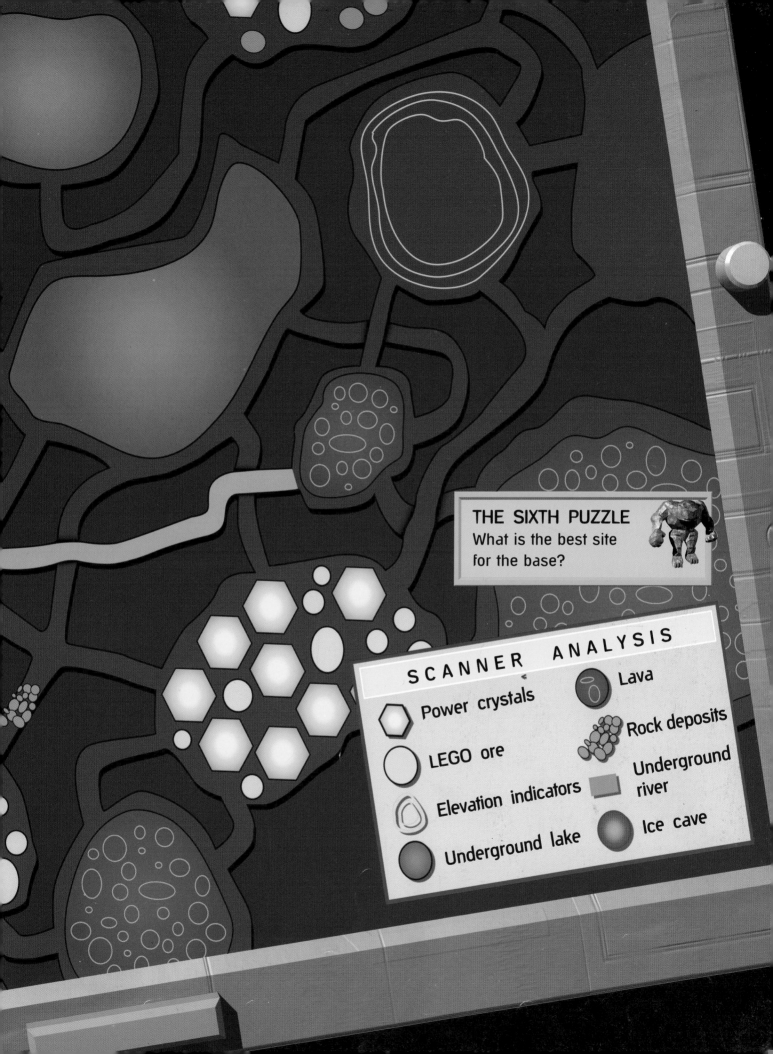

THE SIXTH PUZZLE
What is the best site
for the base?

SCANNER ANALYSIS

Power crystals

LEGO ore

Elevation indicators

Underground lake

Lava

Rock deposits

Underground river

Ice cave

Axle sat at the controls of the Giant Drilling Vehicle, while Sparks directed from the ground. They had just extracted a rock containing precious power crystals.

Suddenly, they heard an angry roar! The ground shook as a mob of Rock Monsters thundered toward them. Sparks stepped back in terror . . . and disappeared!

Axle scrambled out of the GDV. "Sparks? Sparks?"

"Down here. I need some help. Quick!"

Sparks had fallen down to the bottom of a ravine. The Rock Monsters were advancing on him! Luckily, Axle remembered their previous meeting with a Rock Monster. He had an idea.

THE SEVENTH PUZZLE
What does Axle remember that will help Sparks?

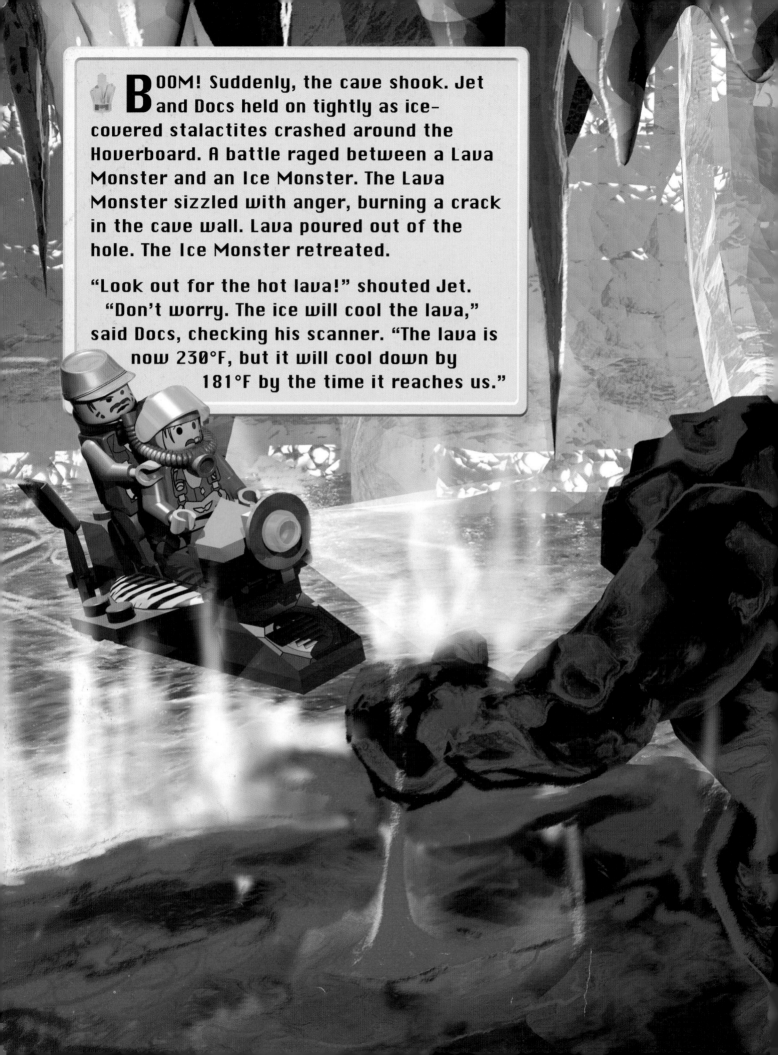

BOOM! Suddenly, the cave shook. Jet and Docs held on tightly as ice-covered stalactites crashed around the Hoverboard. A battle raged between a Lava Monster and an Ice Monster. The Lava Monster sizzled with anger, burning a crack in the cave wall. Lava poured out of the hole. The Ice Monster retreated.

"Look out for the hot lava!" shouted Jet. "Don't worry. The ice will cool the lava," said Docs, checking his scanner. "The lava is now 230°F, but it will cool down by 181°F by the time it reaches us."

THE EIGHTH PUZZLE
What will the temperature of the lava be when it reaches the Hoverboard?

The Rock Raiders got back from their expeditions and moved the equipment to the site Docs and Jet had found for their Underground Headquarters.

Docs studied the chart. "Deposits of both power crystals and LEGO ore lie just south of here."

"Jackpot!" said Bandit. "We'll take it all back to the Explorer, then we'll head for home."

"It's a bit harder than that," said Docs. "The LEGO ore is buried deep beneath the surface."

THE NINTH PUZZLE
What elements must the Rock Raiders
drill through to reach the LEGO ore?
Clue: Find the key to the elements.

SEARCHING: LEGO ore

Axle was using the Giant Drilling Vehicle to drill for LEGO ore when Docs detected a problem.

"Stop drilling!" he called. "The scanner shows a layer of dangerous gas blocking the path to the ore. If we drill directly into the gas, we'll cause a massive explosion!"

Docs relayed the facts to the Chief on the Explorer.

"Only water will stabilize the gas," came the Chief's reply.

"There are about 100 gallons of water under the surface," said Bandit, looking at the scanner. "But is that enough?"

DANGER - explosive gas

THE TENTH PUZZLE
It takes one gallon of water to stabilize ten gallons of the gas. There are 850 gallons of gas surrounding the LEGO ore – is there enough water to stop an explosion?

After drilling for the LEGO ore, the Rock Raiders located the power crystals. They were buried in a heap of granite boulders.

They needed two rocks full of crystals to power the drills and dig out the richest crystal deposit on the planet. Jet set off in the Tunnel Transporter and found two rocks full of crystals.

Suddenly, a volcano blasted hot lava up into the cave. The force threw Jet to the ground, knocking her unconscious.

When she woke, Jet was surrounded by lava. The volcano had flung her crystals right in the middle of the lava.

THE ELEVENTH PUZZLE
How can Jet safely cross the lava to retrieve the crystals and then return to the Tunnel Transporter?

At last, Jet returned with the vital power crystals. The Rock Raiders continued drilling, and soon they reached the last layer of granite boulders. They switched to laser drills, but the final boulders would not budge.

"We'll have to use explosives to reach that deposit of power crystals," said Axle. "But too big an explosion will bring the boulders right down on top of us."

Docs used his scanner to calculate. "At this density each boulder will take six pounds of explosive to move," he said.

THE TWELFTH PUZZLE
How much explosive must they use to move all of the boulders?

The explosion ripped through the granite boulders to reveal an enormous pile of rocks with power crystals glittering inside.

Now there were enough crystals for the Rock Raiders and for the Monsters, too.

Just then, there was a message from the Explorer. The Chief's voice sounded faint. "Power is failing. We need power crystals urgently. Send them on the teleport platform..." Then the Rock Raiders lost contact.

"The blast has completely destroyed our teleport platform," said Docs. "But," he added quickly, "we've still got all the parts, and I have the plans to help us rebuild it."

THE THIRTEENTH PUZZLE
There are three LEGO pieces in this picture that are **not** needed to build the teleport platform. Which are they?

With the teleport platform, the Rock Raiders quickly transported the power crystals and LEGO ore up to the LMS Explorer. The crew were very glad to see them.

"Well done! Mission Rock Raiders has been successful," the Chief announced. "We have more than enough crystals to power our homeward journey and enough LEGO ore to carry out repairs to the ship."

But the Chief's speech was interrupted by a warning from the ship's scanner: "Warning. Alien present on deck."

"An alien?!" The Rock Raiders sprang into action.

THE FINAL PUZZLE
Can you spot the alien?

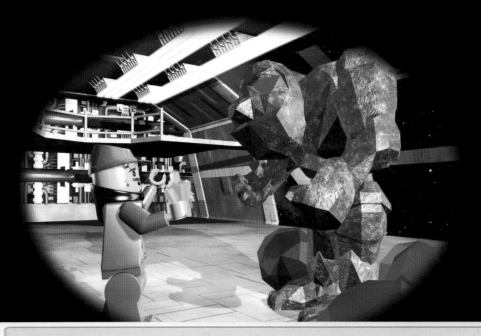

o one could find the alien. Then suddenly, there it was in front of them — a very big, very hungry Rock Monster!

"I hope we've got enough crystals to feed this guy," gulped Docs. "Otherwise, we're in trouble!"

MORE ROCK RAIDER PUZZLES

1 On the Rock Raider scanners, what color represents granite?

2 Which vehicle can transport the entire Rock Raider team and their equipment underground?

3 Stalactites are limestone deposits which drip down from cave roofs. Stalagmites grow upward from the cave floor. How many stalactites can you find in the book?

4 What would the Rock Raiders encounter if they drilled down from their Underground Headquarters through the deposit of LEGO ore, and then drilled toward the southeast?

ANSWERS: 1. granite - purple; 2. Tunnel Transporter; 3. 27; 4. lava

ANSWERS

THE FIRST PUZZLE
The scanners have found LEGO ore at 8,000 miles and power crystals at 4,000 miles.

THE SECOND PUZZLE
Five Rock Raiders can be transported to the planet.

THE THIRD PUZZLE
The Tunnel Transporter travels at a speed of 0.2 miles per second.
[Speed = distance (2 miles) divided by the time (10 seconds) = 0.2 miles per second]

THE FOURTH PUZZLE

THE FIFTH PUZZLE

THE SIXTH PUZZLE

There are five power crystals.

THE SEVENTH PUZZLE
Axle remembers that Rock Monsters like to eat power crystals, so Sparks should give them his crystals.

THE EIGHTH PUZZLE
The temperature of the lava when it reaches the Hoverboard will be 49°F.

THE NINTH PUZZLE
They must drill through the outer surface, granite, power crystals, and volcanic rock.
(The key to the elements can be found on Spread 1.)

THE TENTH PUZZLE
Yes – 100 gallons of water stabilizes 1000 gallons of gas.

THE ELEVENTH PUZZLE

THE TWELTH PUZZLE
12 boulders x 6 pounds each = 72 pounds.

THE THIRTEENTH PUZZLE
These bricks are not needed to make the teleport platform:

FINAL PUZZLE

A DK PUBLISHING BOOK
www.dk.com
First American Edition, 1999
2 4 6 8 10 9 7 5 3

Published in the United States by DK Publishing, Inc.
95 Madison Avenue, New York, New York, 10016

Text © 1999 LEGO Group
Illustrations © 1999 LEGO Group
Designers: Nick Avery and John Kelly
Editor: Caryn Jenner
Managing Art Editor: Cathy Tincknell
Managing Editor: Joanna Devereux
Copyright © 1999 Dorling Kindersley Limited, London.

DK Publishing books are available at special discounts for bulk purchases for sales promotions or premiums.
Special edtions, including personalized covers, excerpts of existing guides, and corporate imprints can be created in
large quantities for specific needs. For more information, contact Special Markets Dept., DK Publishing, Inc, 95 Madison Avenue,
New York, NY 10016, Fax: 800-600-9098.

ISBN 0-7894-4707-X
Color reproduction by Dot Gradations
Printed and bound in Italy by L.E.G.O.